I Can't Believe *THAT'S* Healthy!

SURI GANZ

I Can't Believe THAT's Healthy!
© 2016 The Judaica Press, Inc.

ISBN: 978-1-60763-230-6

Editor: Nechoma Leshinsky
Proofreaders: Raizy Rosenzweig, Hadassa Goldsmith
Designer: Lasso Design

THE JUDAICA PRESS, INC.
123 Ditmas Avenue / Brooklyn, NY 11218
718-972-6200 / 800-972-6201
info@judaicapress.com
www.judaicapress.com

Manufactured in China

Foreword

I have been a personal trainer for the past 20 years and have trained hundreds of clients ranging from ages 9 to 89. While they all had different goals when it came to training, the one goal they all shared was the desire to eat healthier. I noticed that while there are amazing cooks out there, when it comes to healthy eating most people are clueless. To help my clients, over the years I have created delicious, healthy, original and easy recipes so they could live a healthy lifestyle without feeling deprived or bored. As a result, I've been asked many times to come out with a cookbook.

Eventually, I listened.

The cookbook you have been waiting for is finally here. Now anyone who wants healthy, easy-to-prepare delicious food can have this cookbook at their fingertips.

The reason this project took so many years to launch was the tremendous work involved. I was truly fortunate to have had many wonderful people as part of my team helping me from beginning to end.

My children Brochie, Elly, Duvie, Moishe and Shloime — I want to thank you all for your involvement in this challenging project. Thank you for being my tasters, my critics and my cheerleaders. Shloime, your creativity and handiness were a huge help with the photography. A very special thank you to my son Moishe who dedicated his last free summer to help me shop, cook, taste, edit ... and anything else that was needed. Without you this cookbook would have taken a lot longer to finish.

My parents, in-laws and siblings — Thank you for your support and for sharing all the highs and lows that come with putting together a cookbook. A special thanks to my mother who is the original healthy cook. Her delicious cooking has given me my love of healthy food.

Chef Karen — Thank you to my best friend, who — lucky for me — is also an amazing chef. I would need a whole page to properly thank Karen, but I will try to restrain myself. From the beginning Karen was always there for me, whether it was technical advice, emotional support or — my least favorite — constructive criticism. There were days she would spend hours typing, tasting and even plating some of the dishes for the photography. I could not have done this without her. Thank you, Karen, for all your time and energy. You are a true friend.

Deena Rosenbluth — Thank you to my good friend Deena for all your wonderful recipe contributions. Great minds don't just think alike — they also eat alike.

Raizy Rosenzweig — Thank you to my good friend Raizy. Your extreme patience and meticulousness are the perfect recipe for a very methodical proofreader. Lucky for me I have such capable friends.

Yitzy Gruen — Thank you, Yitzy, for all your patience and time, for helping me navigate the wonderful world of kosher cookbooks, and for helping me become a part of it.

Judaica Press — Thank you for the opportunity to bring my dream to fruition. Nachum Shapiro, Aryeh Mezei and the whole Judaica Press team were a pleasure and an honor to work with.

My husband Shuli — Last but not least, I want to thank my wonderful husband Shuli. Your creativity and perfectionism are the driving forces behind much of the beautiful photography. While I didn't always appreciate these qualities (2½ hours just on one picture!), I definitely appreciate the final results. Thank you for your endless time with helping me on the computer at all times of day or night. Most importantly, thank you for all your support from start to finish.

Since the issue of whether you need to check various types of fruits and vegetables for insects and precisely how to do so is somewhat complex, please consult your Rabbi. However, please note that for any recipe that calls for a vegetable that is available in both fresh and frozen forms, you can use the frozen variety just as well as fresh.

Contents

APPETIZERS/DIPS   **11**

Baked Onion Rings 12

Mango Tomato Platter 14

Baked Zucchini Sticks 16

Cheesy Spinach Bites...............................16

Broccoli Cheese Casserole 17

Baked Vegetable Patties 18

Eggplant Parmesan 20

Squash Tomato Casserole 21

Italian Cheesy Baked Vegetables.............22

Portabella Pizza......................................24

Zoodles (Zucchini Noodles) with
    Chunky Tomato and Garlic Sauce 26

Rutabaga Latkes 28

Ranch Dill Dip 30

Leek Dip 32

Smoky Babaganoush................................33

Roasted Pepper Garlic Dip 33

Tomato Salsa..34

SALADS   **35**

Tropical Salad...36

Avocado Salad 38

Marinated Baby Corn Salad 40

Bistro Salad 42

Chickpea Pepper Salad 43

Blueberry Feta Cheese Salad 44

Chopped Veggie Burger Salad 46

Crunchy Salad 47

Carrot Apple Salad 48

Citrus Beet Salad 50

Cucumber Radish Salad 52

Health Salad 53

Hearts of Palm Mango Salad................... 54

Hearts of Palm and Asparagus Salad 56

Jicama Salad 57

Orange and Water Chestnut Salad 58

Lentil Salad.. 60

Mock Potato Salad.................................. 61

Sesame Quinoa Salad 62

Oriental Salad 64

Red and Green Cabbage Salad 65

Spanish Salad..66

Spinach and Plum Salad..........................68

Spinach Rainbow Salad with Thai
    Dressing 69

Sunshine Salad 70

Sweet and Savory Salmon Salad 71

Carrot Blueberry Salad 72

Honey Mustard Spring Salad....................74

Strawberry Tomato Basil Salad 75

Pesto Tuna Salad.................................... 76

Turkey Spring Salad 77

SLAWS   79

Broccoli Mango Slaw 80

California Slaw 81

Red Cabbage Coleslaw............................. 82

Perfect Diet Coleslaw................................ 84

Russian Coleslaw 85

SOUPS   87

Beet Soup 88

Lean, Green and Supreme Soup 90

Cauliflower Zucchini Soup 91

Butternut Squash and Pear Soup 92

Cauliflower and Smokey Pepper Soup 94

Chunky Tuscan Tomato Soup 96

Cream of Mushroom Soup 98

Hungarian Cherry Soup 99

Chunky Vegetable Soup 100

Creamy Winter White Soup..................... 102

Crockpot Butternut Squash Soup........... 104

Cucumber Soup 106

Velvety Pea Soup 108

Pumpkin Soup 110

Roasted Cauliflower Leek Soup.............. 112

Tomato Soup with Shredded Zucchini..... 113

Tomato Quinoa Soup............................... 114

Zucchini Soup.. 116

SIDE DISHES   119

Assorted Roasted Vegetables 120

Eggplant Medley 121

Butternut Squash Risotto 122

Broccoli and Brussels Sprouts................. 124

Butternut Squash Hash Browns 125

Candied Butternut Squash...................... 126

Chinese Vegetables................................. 128

Nicer Dicer Chopped Zucchini and
    Mushrooms.. 129

Celery Root and Parsnip Mash............... 130

Garlic Broccoli with Cream Sauce 132

Garlic Eggplant 133

Eggplant Ratatouille 134

Honey Glazed String Beans.................... 136

Hot and Spicy Brussels Sprouts 137

Hot and Spicy Cauliflower 138

Lemon Garlic Asparagus 140

Tangy Portabella Mushrooms with
    Roasted Red Peppers....................... 141

Marsala Mushrooms................................ 142

Cauliflower Rice 144

Roasted Garlic Cauliflower...................... 145

Roasted Maple Brussels Sprouts............ 146

Roasted Sesame Asparagus.................... 148

Rutabaga French Fries............................ 150

Sautéed Spinach 152

Sautéed Vegetables and Quinoa 153

Sugar Snap Peas with Mushrooms 154

Sesame Celery 156

Sesame Zoodles...................................... 157

Sundried Tomatoes.................................. 158

Shredded Kohlrabi and Carrots.............. 160

Sweet and Sour Cabbage....................... 160

Sweet and Sour Vegetables 161

Tomato and Basil Spinach 162

Sweet and Spicy Carrot Fries 164

Citrus Shredded Carrots 165

Matchstick Vegetables 166
Tzimmes 167
Zucchini in Tomato Sauce 168

KUGELS   **169**
Broccoli Lukshen Kugel............................ 170
Butternut Squash Kugel 171
California Kugel..172
Cauliflower Kugel 173
Cauliflower Butternut Squash Kugel........174
Pineapple Noodle Kugel 176
Pumpkin Pineapple Kugel 178
Zucchini Kugel 180
Shredded Apple Kugel 182
Spinach "Lukshen" Kugel......................... 184

SNACKS   **185**
Baked Apple Chips 186
Carrot Crisps 188
Chocolate Halva Treats 189
Blueberry Chia Pudding 190
Cinnamon Apple Snack............................192
Coconut Pineapple Kisses........................ 193
Dairy-free Peanut Butter Cups 194
Scrumptious Chocolate Chip Cookies 196
Melt-in-Your-Mouth Brownies 197
Fat-Free Apple Cinnamon Muffins 198
Low-carb Almond Cookies 200
Vanilla Meringue Cookies 202
Sweet Potato Chips 204

DESSERTS   **207**
Apple Meringue.......................................208
Apple Pear Crisp..................................... 209
Apple Pie with Biscotti Crumbs............... 210
Banana Cake...212
Blueberry Apple Pie 213
Apple Strudel..214
Crustless Strawberry Cream Pie..............216
Honey-Drizzled Peaches with
     Crunchy Oat Topping 217
Mango Ices 218
Pina Colada Granita 220
Plum Tart..221
Rich and Creamy Chocolate Mousse...... 222
Strawberry Mousse 224
Strawberry Blueberry "Pie".....................226
Strawberry Rhubarb Compote 227
Vanilla Fudge Ice Cream..........................228
Mini Sweet Potato Soufflés.....................230

Appetizers/Dips

Baked Onion Rings

SERVES 2-4

1–2 Vidalia onions, cut into ½ inch slices, separated into 12 rings
½ c. whole wheat bread crumbs
¼ c. wheat germ
½ tsp. chili powder
½ tsp. onion powder
½ tsp. salt
½ tsp. garlic powder
½ tsp. paprika
4 egg whites, beaten
Cooking spray

Preheat oven to 375°. Place bread crumbs, wheat germ and spices in a small wide bowl. Toss together. Beat egg whites in another small wide bowl. Dip each onion ring into egg whites, then into crumb mixture. Grease a cookie sheet with cooking spray. Place dipped onions on the cookie sheet and spray top of onion rings with cooking spray. Bake for 10 minutes, then flip onion rings over and bake for an additional 10 minutes.

For when your mouth says "takeout" but your scale disagrees!

Mango Tomato Platter

SERVES 6

2 beefsteak tomatoes, cut into rounds
1 Kirby with peel on, thinly sliced into rounds
½ red onion, sliced into rings
1 mango, peeled and chopped

Dressing:
3 T. oil
1 T. lemon juice
½ tsp. hot sauce
1 tsp. honey
¼ tsp. garlic powder
Salt and pepper, to taste

Layer tomatoes on the outer rim of a platter. Then, layer Kirby slices inward, toward the middle of the platter, slightly overlapping tomatoes. Layer onion rings, slightly overlapping Kirby rounds. Place mango in center of the platter. In a small bowl, mix dressing ingredients together. Using a spoon, drizzle dressing over platter.

Baked Zucchini Sticks

SERVES 4-6

1 lg. zucchini, cut into approx. 24 sticks
1 T. ranch style soup and dip mix
Cooking spray

Preheat oven to 400°. Place zucchini sticks in a 9x13-inch pan. Spray with cooking spray. Sprinkle with ranch style soup mix. Spray again, then bake uncovered for about 30 minutes or until soft.

Cheesy Spinach Bites

YIELD: 12

2½ c. frozen chopped spinach, defrosted and drained
1 (8 oz.) can mushrooms, drained
1 plum tomato, chopped
2 egg whites
¾ c. shredded low-fat cheese
¼ tsp. onion powder
¼ tsp. garlic pepper
¼ tsp. salt

Preheat oven to 350°. In a large bowl, mix all ingredients. Spoon mixture into 2 muffin pans (totaling 12 spinach bites). Bake for 30 minutes.

Broccoli Cheese Casserole

SERVES 4

½ c. shredded low-fat cheese
1 c. cooked brown rice
1 (8 oz.) can mushrooms, drained
1 T. onion soup mix (no MSG)
Salt and pepper, to taste
1 (16 oz.) bag broccoli florets, chopped

Preheat oven to 350°. Place ingredients (except broccoli) in a medium pot on small flame. Cook until cheese is melted and then add broccoli. Mix together. Place in a 9-inch round dish. Bake for 20 minutes, uncovered.

This is a great dish for when you want to eat light and meatless.
The combination of the rice, broccoli and cheese makes it a complete meal.

Baked Vegetable Patties

YIELD: 6

1 onion, chopped
2 stalks celery, chopped
2 c. cubed butternut squash, cooked
1 (15 oz.) can mushrooms, drained
1 egg
¼ tsp. pepper
¼ tsp. onion powder
¼ tsp. garlic powder
¼ tsp. salt
Cooking spray

Sauté onion, celery, butternut squash and mushrooms until onions and celery are soft. Let cool and place in a bowl. Add egg and spices and combine. Grease a cookie sheet with cooking spray. Form patties and place on the greased cookie sheet. Bake at 350° for 40 minutes.

Eggplant Parmesan

SERVES 4-6

1 lg. eggplant
2 egg whites
½ tsp. salt
2 T. whole wheat bread crumbs
1 (15 oz.) can pizza sauce (or tomato sauce)
10 oz. frozen chopped broccoli, defrosted
1 c. 70-calorie shredded mozzarella
Cooking spray

Leaving the peel on, slice eggplant very thinly. Grease a cookie sheet with cooking spray. Dip eggplant into egg whites. Place on the cookie sheet. Sprinkle salt and bread crumbs on top and then spray eggplant with cooking spray. Broil for 5-7 minutes until soft. Pour ⅓ of tomato sauce into a 9x13-inch pan. Spread with a spoon, then place ½ of eggplant slices, then ½ of broccoli and ½ of cheese. Repeat layering process, ending with cheese on top. Bake at 350° uncovered for about 30 minutes until cheese is melted.

This recipe tastes just as good as the pizza shop version but it comes guilt-free!

Squash Tomato Casserole

SERVES 4

Low-calorie | Low-fat | Gluten-free | Vegan | Dairy-free | Passover

½ green squash, sliced into rounds
½ yellow squash, sliced into rounds
3 plum tomatoes, sliced into rounds
1 red onion, sliced into rounds

Vinaigrette:
¼ c. oil
Juice of ½ fresh lemon
1 garlic cube
1 basil cube
1 parsley cube
¼ tsp. garlic pepper
¼ tsp. onion powder
¼ tsp. salt

Preheat oven to 350°. In a small bowl, mix the vinaigrette ingredients. Place green and yellow squash overlapping in a 9-inch round pan. Drizzle 1 T. of vinaigrette on top. Place tomatoes on top of squash. Drizzle 1 T. of vinaigrette on top. Place onions on top of tomatoes. Drizzle remaining dressing on top. Bake covered for 35 minutes, and uncovered for another 20 minutes.

Italian Cheesy Baked Vegetables

SERVES 6

1 Spanish onion, chopped
2 sm. zucchini, chopped
1 lg. eggplant, cubed
1 red pepper, chopped
½ c. cooked chickpeas
1 garlic cube
1 basil cube
¼ tsp. paprika
¼ tsp. onion powder
¼ tsp. crushed red pepper flakes
¼ tsp. salt
2 oz. low-fat shredded cheese
Cooking spray

Grease a 9-inch round pan with cooking spray. Sauté onion, zucchini, eggplant and red pepper in a pan for 2-3 minutes. Add chickpeas, garlic, basil, and spices to the pan. Cook on medium flame until soft. Transfer to the 9-inch round pan. Sprinkle with cheese. Bake at 350° uncovered for 5-7 minutes until cheese melts.

Portabella Pizza

SERVES 6

6 lg. portabella mushroom caps, peeled and cleaned
6 thin slices beefsteak tomato
6 T. tomato sauce
¼ tsp. basil
¼ tsp. oregano
½ c. (2 oz.) 70-calorie low-fat cheese, divided

Place mushroom caps in a 9x13-inch pan. Place one tomato slice and 1 T. tomato sauce in each cap. Sprinkle with basil and oregano, and top with cheese. Cover with foil, and bake at 350° for 20 minutes. Uncover and bake for an additional 10 minutes.

Any recipe with pizza in its name doesn't need a description ....

Zoodles (Zucchini Noodles) with Chunky Tomato and Garlic Sauce

SERVES 4-6

2 green zucchini, with peel
1 yellow zucchini, with peel
1 T. olive oil
5 garlic cloves
5 basil cubes
5 plum tomatoes, chopped
Salt and pepper, to taste

Use a Julienne peeler to make strands of zucchini noodles. Set aside. Heat a skillet and add olive oil, garlic, basil and tomatoes. On medium flame, cook until liquid from tomatoes evaporates. Lower flame; add zucchini noodles, salt and pepper to the skillet, stir into sauce, and mix for one minute.

If you are gluten-free or following a low-carb diet and you are a pasta person, you will love this dish! It's delicious and easy to make. There are a lot of inexpensive easy tools on the market, like a spiralizer or a veggeti, but if you don't have any of these you can just use a Julienne peeler.

Rutabaga Latkes

YIELD: 6

1 lg. rutabaga
½ Spanish onion
1 T. + 1 tsp. oil
2 eggs plus 2 egg whites
½ T. salt
¼ tsp. paprika
Cooking spray

Place rutabaga in microwave for 5 minutes. (This will not cook it but will make it easier to work with.) Peel rutabaga, then cut into 4–6 large pieces. Using a grater disc, grate rutabaga pieces and onion. Place in a large bowl. Grease a large Teflon skillet with cooking spray. Add oil and heat on medium flame. Add rest of ingredients to the bowl, squeezing out excess liquid. When oil is very hot, spoon batter into the skillet. Cook on each side for about 5 minutes. Spray the skillet in between batches. (Handle gently so they won't fall apart.)

They say necessity is the mother of invention. In this case, latkes for Chanukah were the necessity and rutabaga the invention. Once you make these, you will realize they are too good to make only once a year.

Ranch Dill Dip

SERVES 6

1 6 oz. container plain Greek yogurt
1 T. grated Parmesan cheese
1 T. ranch mix
1 T. fresh dill, finely chopped
½ tsp. garlic powder

Mix ingredients in a small bowl until texture is smooth. Serve with vegetables or use as dressing for salad.

Leek Dip

SERVES 8

Low-calorie Low-fat Low-carb Gluten-free Dairy-free Passover

6 garlic cloves
3 leeks
½ c. light mayonnaise
½ c. water
¼ tsp. garlic pepper
Salt, to taste
Cooking spray

Place 6 garlic cloves in silver foil, spray garlic with cooking spray and seal tightly. Bake in oven at 450° for 30 minutes. Chop leeks (using only white and light green parts). Sauté leeks in cooking spray for 2 minutes. Place all ingredients in a food processor and blend until smooth.

Smoky Babaganoush

SERVES 6

1 lg. eggplant
2 T. tehina paste
1 garlic cube
Juice of 1 fresh lemon
Salt, to taste

Place eggplant on oven floor. (If you don't like a smoky flavor, you can bake on a rack.) Bake for 1 hour at 400°. Let cool. Scoop eggplant from peel. Place in a food processor and add rest of ingredients. Blend until it has a smooth consistency.

Roasted Pepper Garlic Dip

SERVES 6

12 oz. jar roasted peppers, drained
3 T. light mayonnaise
2 garlic cubes
¼ tsp. salt
¼ tsp. garlic pepper

Blend all ingredients together in a food processor until smooth.

Tomato Salsa

SERVES 6-8

6 plum tomatoes, diced
½ red onion, diced
1 jalapeño pepper, seeded and chopped
1 garlic cube
1½ tsp. dried oregano
½ tsp. salt
¼ tsp. pepper
1 T. fresh lemon juice
1 T. fresh lime juice

Combine all ingredients in a large bowl. Mix well, and then cover tightly. Refrigerate for a minimum of 2 hours before serving.

Salads

Tropical Salad

SERVES 2

1 Kirby cucumber
1 red pepper
½ c. jicama
1 c. pineapple chunks

Dressing:
2 T. sesame oil
½ tsp. soy sauce
2 T. orange juice
½ tsp. garlic powder
1 tsp. red wine vinegar
1 packet sweetener
Salt and pepper, to taste

Topping:
¼ c. cashew pieces
1 T. black sesame seeds

Cut Kirby, red pepper and jicama into strips. Place vegetables and pineapple in a medium bowl. Mix dressing ingredients in a small bowl. Pour dressing over salad. Top with cashews and black sesame seeds.

Avocado Salad

SERVES 4

1 on-the-vine tomato
¼ red onion
2 ripe avocados

Dressing:
2 T. olive oil
1 T. red wine vinegar
¼ tsp. garlic pepper
¼ tsp. salt
1 packet sweetener

Cut tomatoes into chunks and place in a bowl. Thinly slice onion into ½ rings and add to the bowl. Mix dressing ingredients and pour over vegetables. Peel and chop avocados, and then add to the bowl. Toss and serve.

The first time I tried this salad was at a wedding. I don't remember the couple, but the salad and I were a match made in heaven!

Marinated Baby Corn Salad

SERVES 8-10

1 (15 oz.) can baby corn pieces

1 (16 oz.) pkg. frozen sugar snap peas, defrosted

1 green pepper, cut into strips

1 red pepper, cut into strips

1 yellow pepper, cut into strips

1 orange pepper, cut into strips

1 sm. red onion, cut into half rings

Dressing:

3 T. oil

6 T. water

Salt and pepper, to taste

2 T. sweetener

1 tsp. vinegar

Place all vegetables in a large bowl. Mix dressing ingredients, pour over vegetables, and marinate for 3 hours or overnight.

Bistro Salad

SERVES 4

Low-calorie · Low-fat · Gluten-free · Vegan · Dairy-free · Passover

6 portabella mushrooms, cut into halves
1 red pepper, cut into strips
Salt, to taste
Cooking spray
1 (9 oz.) bag romaine lettuce
1 lg. carrot, shredded
8 black olives, cut into halves

Dressing:
2 T. oil
2 tsp. balsamic vinegar
1 packet sweetener
Salt and pepper, to taste

Place mushrooms and pepper strips in a 9-inch round pan. Sprinkle with salt and spray with cooking spray. Broil for 15 minutes (until skin of pepper is charred). Place lettuce and carrot in a medium bowl and toss. Cool vegetables and place on top of salad. Garnish with olives. Combine dressing ingredients and drizzle on salad. Mix well.

Chickpea Pepper Salad

SERVES 4

1 green pepper, finely diced

1 yellow pepper, finely diced

1 red pepper, finely diced

½ red onion, diced

1 c. chickpeas, cooked (canned or fresh)

Dressing:

2 T. oil

Juice of ½ fresh lemon

Salt and pepper, to taste

Mix vegetables and chickpeas in a bowl. Add dressing ingredients and mix well.

Blueberry Feta Cheese Salad

SERVES 2

1 (9 oz.) bag romaine lettuce
¼ red onion, sliced into half rings
2 T. nuts
4 oz. feta cheese
1 c. fresh blueberries

Put lettuce in a bowl. Place remaining ingredients on top of lettuce.

Dressing:
2 T. sugar-free blueberry jelly
2 T. light mayonnaise
Juice of ½ fresh lemon

Mix dressing ingredients until smooth. Pour over salad.

Who needs to go out for lunch? The combination of sweet and salty makes a salad that hits the spot, and it will have you counting down the minutes until your lunch break.

Chopped Veggie Burger Salad

SERVES 2-4

1 box mushrooms, peeled and sliced
½ lg. Vidalia onion, chopped
1 (10 oz.) bag salad mix (I use Italian blend)
4 veggie burgers, cut into pieces
1 lg. sour pickle, chopped
1 plum tomato, chopped
Cooking spray

Dressing:
3 T. light mayonnaise
1 T. low sugar ketchup
Juice of 1 fresh lemon
¼ tsp. salt
¼ tsp. garlic powder

Using cooking spray, sauté mushrooms and chopped onion in a skillet. Let cool. Place all ingredients in a large bowl and mix. Combine dressing ingredients. Pour over salad.

Crunchy Salad

SERVES 4-6

10 stalks celery, diced

8 oz. baby carrots, diced

1 lg. red pepper, diced

⅓ c. red onion, diced

Dressing:

1/4 c. light mayonnaise

2 T. oil

1 tsp. red wine vinegar

1 squirt of mustard

1 T. honey

Salt and pepper, to taste

Mix salad ingredients in a large bowl. Mix dressing ingredients and toss until salad is well coated.

Carrot Apple Salad

SERVES 4

2 lg. carrots, shredded
1 green apple, shredded
1 red apple, shredded
3 T. sunflower seeds
3 T. craisins

Dressing:
3 T. light mayonnaise
2 tsp. lemon juice
3 packets sweetener
¼ tsp. salt

Mix salad ingredients in a medium bowl. Mix dressing ingredients, pour over salad and toss.

Citrus Beet Salad

SERVES 6

1 (15 oz.) can sliced beets
¼ red onion, chopped

Dressing:
1 tsp. olive oil
1 packet sweetener
Juice of ½ a lime
Juice of ½ an orange
Juice of ½ fresh lemon

Dice beets into thin sticks. Place beets and chopped onion in a medium bowl. Mix dressing ingredients, pour over salad and toss.

I created this recipe for Rosh Hashanah to use as one of the simanim. To my surprise, my son-in-law loved it and finished the whole bowl.

Cucumber Radish Salad

SERVES 6

6 Persian cucumbers

8 radishes

1 red onion

½ T. salt

1 c. water

2 tsp. red wine vinegar

1 T. pourable sweetener

Using the slicing blade of a food processor, cut cucumbers, radishes and red onion. Put sliced vegetables in a medium bowl and sprinkle with salt. Let stand for 30 minutes to draw out the water, softening vegetables. Add water, vinegar and sweetener. Toss and place in a tightly sealed container. Put in refrigerator for a minimum of 2 hours to marinate.

The radish adds an extra crunch to ordinary cucumber salad.

Health Salad

SERVES 6-8

1 (14 oz.) bag coleslaw mix
1 lg. carrot
1 red pepper
2 Persian cucumbers
½ red onion

Marinade:
2 c. water
3 T. oil
4 tsp. vinegar
2 tsp. salt
5 packets sweetener

Place coleslaw mix in a large bowl and set aside. Shred carrot in a food processor and add to coleslaw mix. Slice rest of ingredients in food processor (this can also be done by hand but must be sliced thinly), and add to the bowl. Prepare marinade and pour over salad. Let stand for several hours.

I have tried many different versions of store-bought health salad, but I didn't like any of them. So I created my own – and now you can enjoy it, too!

Hearts of Palm Mango Salad

SERVES 4

1 (15 oz.) can hearts of palm
1 sm. green pepper, chopped
1 mango, peeled and chopped
¼ red onion, thinly sliced into half rings

Dressing:
1 T. oil
1 packet sweetener
1 tsp. red wine vinegar
Salt, to taste

Topping:
1 T. craisins

In a medium bowl, place hearts of palm, green pepper, mango and red onion. Mix dressing ingredients and add to salad. Top salad with craisins.

Hearts of Palm and Asparagus Salad

SERVES 4

20 spears fresh asparagus
1 (15 oz.) can hearts of palm
1¼ c. grape tomatoes
3 scallions

Dressing:
3 T. olive oil
1 T. red wine vinegar
2 basil cubes
2 garlic cubes
Juice of ½ fresh lemon
2 packets sweetener
Salt and pepper, to taste

Trim and chop asparagus, place in pan, and broil for 20 minutes. Meanwhile, slice hearts of palm, grape tomatoes and scallions, and place in a medium bowl. Add cooked asparagus. Mix dressing ingredients, pour over salad and toss.

This is a more sophisticated version of the regular hearts of palm salad recipes.

Jicama Salad

SERVES 6-8

1 (10 oz.) bag romaine lettuce
1 jicama, peeled and cut into sticks
1 (15 oz.) can hearts of palm, cut into circles

Dressing:
⅓ c. olive oil
1 T. grated Spanish onion
3 packets sweetener
1 tsp. vinegar
½ tsp. dry mustard
Salt, to taste
1 tsp. poppy seeds

Topping:
⅓ c. pomegranate seeds

Place lettuce, jicama and hearts of palm in a large bowl. Mix dressing ingredients and pour over salad. Top with pomegranate seeds.

This recipe comes from my friend Chanie. She says it's a family favorite — after tasting it, I can see why!

Orange and Water Chestnut Salad

SERVES 2

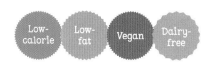

1 (8 oz.) can sliced water chestnuts, drained
1 Kirby, peeled and chopped
1 navel orange, peeled and cut into small pieces
½ med. red onion, sliced into half rings

Dressing:
1 T. oil
1 parsley cube
1 basil cube
½ tsp. red wine vinegar
1 T. orange juice
1 packet sweetener

Topping:
2 T. sunflower seeds

Mix salad ingredients in a medium bowl. In a small bowl, mix dressing. Mix dressing ingredients, pour over salad and toss. Top with sunflower seeds.

Lentil Salad

SERVES 8

1 c. lentils, cooked in pareve chicken flavor or vegetable stock
½ c. shredded carrots
1 cooked parsnip, cubed
¼ c. chopped scallion
1 (10 oz.) bag mixed salad greens

Dressing:
3 T. olive oil
½ tsp. balsamic vinegar
1 garlic cube
1 parsley cube
Salt and pepper, to taste

In a large bowl, toss lentils, carrots, parsnip, chopped scallion and salad greens. Mix dressing ingredients, pour over salad and toss.

Mock Potato Salad

SERVES 4

4 lg. parsnips, peeled and chopped
1 T. light mayonnaise
1 T. grated carrot
1 tsp. grated red onion
1 tsp. lemon juice
1 packet sweetener
Salt, to taste

Place parsnips in a pot and add water to cover. Cook until soft, about 20 minutes. Drain. Add rest of ingredients and mix well.

I loooooooooooove (okay, I think you got the picture) potato salad, but I never liked the cauliflower versions. After much experimenting, I came up with this recipe. It tastes so much like potato salad, your family might not be able to tell the difference.

Sesame Quinoa Salad

SERVES 6

1 c. cooked quinoa

½ c. edamame

3 scallions, chopped (white part only)

2 c. angel hair cabbage

Dressing:

1 T. sesame oil

1 T. olive oil

¼ tsp. garlic powder

¼ tsp. salt

1 T. soy sauce (gluten-free)

1 packet sweetener

Mix salad ingredients together in a large bowl. Mix dressing ingredients, pour over salad and toss.

Oriental Salad

SERVES 6

1 (10 oz.) pkg. angel hair coleslaw
½ c. shredded carrots
½ red pepper, cut into thin sticks
1 T. sesame seeds
1 T. sunflower seeds

Dressing:
2 T. light mayonnaise
1 T. sesame oil
½ tsp. soy sauce (gluten-free)
1 garlic cube
¾ tsp. salt

Mix salad ingredients in a bowl. Mix dressing ingredients, pour over salad and toss. (You can substitute regular coleslaw mix for angel hair coleslaw; if so, omit shredded carrots.)

Red and Green Cabbage Salad

SERVES 8-10

1 (14 oz.) bag red cabbage
1 (14 oz.) bag green cabbage
5 scallions, chopped

Dressing:
3 T. light mayonnaise
1 tsp. vinegar
½ tsp. salt
1 T. pourable sweetener
1 basil cube

Topping:
¼ c. pomegranate seeds
2 T. toasted slivered almonds

In a large bowl, mix red and green cabbage and scallions. Mix dressing ingredients, pour over salad and toss. Top salad with pomegranate seeds and slivered almonds.

Spanish Salad

SERVES 4

4 plum tomatoes, chopped
1 Kirby, chopped
3 scallions, chopped (white part only)
8 stuffed olives
2 T. capers
1 (4 oz.) pkg. watercress

Dressing:
2 T. olive oil
1 tsp. red wine vinegar
¼ tsp. cumin
¼ tsp. salt
1 garlic cube
Pinch of black pepper

Place salad ingredients in a medium bowl. Mix dressing ingredients, pour over salad and toss.

Made with watercress, this salad is different and interesting. Add the cumin dressing and it's sensational!

Spinach and Plum Salad

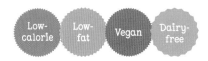

SERVES 8

1 (15 oz.) bag fresh spinach
4 black plums, sliced into wedges
1 (15 oz.) can sliced beets, cut into half circles
½ red onion, cut into half rings
1 avocado, peeled and cut into wedges

Dressing:
1 T. oil
1 T. red wine vinegar
¼ c. lite orange juice
1 tsp. spicy brown mustard
1 tsp. fresh lemon juice
Salt and pepper, to taste

Place salad ingredients in a large bowl. Mix dressing ingredients, pour over salad and toss.

Spinach Rainbow Salad with Thai Dressing

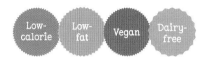

SERVES 4

1 c. shredded carrots

1 (10 oz.) bag fresh spinach

1 c. shredded red cabbage

½ c. edamame

1 red pepper, sliced into strips

1 yellow pepper, sliced into strips

4 scallions, chopped (white part only)

Dressing:

1 T. sesame oil

1 T. water

1 T. honey

¼ tsp. garlic powder

1 tsp. rice vinegar

Salt and pepper, to taste

Mix salad ingredients in a large bowl. Mix dressing ingredients, pour over salad and toss.

Sunshine Salad

SERVES 4

1 avocado, chopped
1 red grapefruit, peeled and chopped
2 peaches, peeled and chopped
1 Kirby, peeled and chopped
2 T. minced red onion
Squeeze of fresh lemon and lime
¼ tsp. salt

Toss ingredients in a medium bowl.

Sweet and Savory Salmon Salad

SERVES 4

1 (6 oz.) bag butter lettuce mix

1 butternut squash, peeled, roasted and cubed

1 green apple, peeled and thinly sliced

½ red onion, cut into rings

1 (7.5 oz.) can salmon

2 T. craisins

2 T. sesame seeds

Dressing:

3 T. light mayonnaise

1 T. sugar-free pancake syrup

Place salad ingredients in a medium bowl. Mix dressing ingredients, pour over salad and toss.

This is one of my favorite salads. It has so many wonderful tastes and textures. The different colors make this extremely appealing as well. Invite your friends over and enjoy — this salad is a meal!

Carrot Blueberry Salad

SERVES 2-4

1 c. blueberries
1 (10 oz.) bag shredded carrots

Dressing:
2 T. oil
¼ tsp. salt
¼ tsp. pepper
Squeeze of fresh lemon

Topping:
2 T. toasted sesame seeds

Combine blueberries and carrots. Mix dressing ingredients and pour over salad.
Sprinkle sesame seeds on top.

Honey Mustard Spring Salad

SERVES 4

1 (5 oz.) bag spring salad mix
4 radishes, cut into slices
1 red pepper, cut into rings
4 scallions, chopped (white part only)

Dressing:
3 T. light mayonnaise
1 tsp. vinegar
2 tsp. honey
1 tsp. mustard
Salt and pepper, to taste

Topping:
3 hard-boiled eggs, sliced

Place salad mix, radishes, pepper and scallions in a medium bowl. Toss together.
Combine dressing ingredients, drizzle over salad and top with eggs.

Strawberry Tomato Basil Salad

SERVES 4

Gluten-free · Low-calorie · Low-fat · Vegan · Dairy-free

1 (10 oz.) bag spinach
1½ c. grape tomatoes, sliced
1 c. strawberries, sliced
1 avocado, peeled and chopped
1 T. shallots, minced
Salt, to taste

Dressing:
2 T. oil
1 tsp. balsamic vinegar
1 packet sweetener

Topping:
2 T. smokehouse almonds

Place spinach in a medium bowl. Add tomatoes, strawberries, avocado, shallots and salt. Mix dressing ingredients, pour over salad and toss. Top with almonds.

Pesto Tuna Salad

SERVES 4

1 (10 oz.) bag romaine lettuce
1 (5 oz.) can tuna in water, drained
1 plum tomato, cut into chunks
1 avocado, peeled and cut into chunks
1 T. capers

Pesto Dressing:
3 garlic cubes
3 basil cubes
1 tsp. oil
1 T. light mayonnaise
Salt and pepper, to taste

Place salad ingredients in a medium bowl. Place garlic, basil and oil in a small bowl and microwave for a few seconds until cubes are thawed. Add mayonnaise, salt and pepper and mix well. Pour over salad.

Turkey Spring Salad

SERVES 2

1 (10 oz.) pkg. of salad greens
6 slices turkey breast, cut into strips
1 c. strawberries, sliced
¼ red onion, sliced

Dressing:
1 T. sugar-free strawberry jelly
1 tsp. red wine vinegar
1 packet sweetener
2 T. light mayonnaise
1 T. unsweetened vanilla almond milk
1 T. water
Salt, to taste

Topping:
3 T. nuts (opt.)

In a large bowl, place salad greens, turkey, strawberries and red onion. Mix dressing ingredients until smooth, pour on salad and top with nuts.

Slaws

Broccoli Mango Slaw

SERVES 2-4

1 (10 oz.) bag broccoli slaw
1 tsp. salt
1 mango, peeled and sliced
10 snow peas, cut into pieces
¼ red onion, chopped

Dressing:
1 T. light mayonnaise
1 tsp. sesame oil
¼ tsp. salt

In a nonstick pan, place broccoli slaw and salt. Sauté for 1–2 minutes. Transfer to a bowl. Add mango, snow peas and red onion. Mix dressing ingredients, pour over salad and toss.

California Slaw

SERVES 6

1 (10 oz.) bag broccoli slaw
1 yellow apple, peeled and cut into matchsticks
1 lg. carrot, shredded
1 jicama, peeled and cut into matchsticks
¼ red onion, chopped

Dressing:
¼ c. light mayonnaise
2 T. honey
1 T. water
1 tsp. mustard
1 tsp. lemon juice
¼ tsp. salt

Topping:
3 T. chopped peanuts

Mix slaw ingredients in a large bowl. Combine dressing ingredients until smooth and pour over slaw. Mix well and top with peanuts.

Red Cabbage Coleslaw

SERVES 6

3 c. shredded red cabbage

2 c. shredded carrots

3 scallions, chopped (white part only)

Dressing:

2 T. light mayonnaise

1 T. Tofutti sour cream supreme

1 tsp. red wine vinegar

2 packets sweetener

½ tsp. celery seeds

1 tsp. oil

2 T. water

Salt and pepper, to taste

Topping:

1 T. sesame seeds

Mix all ingredients in a large bowl. Mix dressing ingredients until blended, pour on cabbage, and top with sesame seeds. Let marinate for 1 hour.

Perfect Diet Coleslaw

SERVES 6

1 (10 oz.) bag angel hair coleslaw
1 lg. carrot, shredded
1 tsp. salt

Dressing:
¼ c. light mayonnaise
1 T. vinegar (gluten-free)
½ c. water
2 T. pourable sweetener

Place coleslaw and carrot in a bowl and sprinkle with salt. Let sit for at least 30 minutes to soften coleslaw. Mix dressing ingredinets, pour over slaw and refrigerate for at least 1 hour. (You can substitute regular coleslaw mix and omit shredded carrots.)

I'm very picky when it comes to diet coleslaw. After trying different techniques and playing with the measurements, I decided this coleslaw is finally fit to grace my Shabbos table.

Russian Coleslaw

SERVES 6

Low-calorie · Low-fat · Sugar-free · Gluten-free · Dairy-free · Passover

5 Kirbies (with peel), diced
¼ red onion, diced
4 red radishes, diced
½ yellow zucchini, diced
½ lg. carrot, peeled and shredded

Dressing:
½ c. light mayonnaise
1 tsp. vinegar (gluten-free)
4 packets sweetener
Salt and pepper, to taste

Place vegetables in a medium bowl. Mix dressing ingredients and pour over coleslaw.

This is great coleslaw to make on Yom Tov when you can't find any coleslaw mix bags at the store because they were all grabbed up, or when you bought a bag of coleslaw mix in advance and now it's spoiled. From now on – problem solved.

Soups

Beet Soup

SERVES 6-8

1 onion, peeled and diced
1 carrot, peeled and diced
1 T. oil
2 lg. beets, peeled and chopped
6 c. pareve chicken flavor or vegetable stock
Salt, to taste

Sauté diced onions and carrots in oil until onions are golden brown. Add beets, stock and salt. Cook on medium flame for approximately 1 hour until beets are soft. Let cool and blend with a stick blender. Serve warm.

*Optional: Stir in 1 tsp. Tofutti sour cream.

Unlike most beet soups, this one is served warm.

Lean, Green and Supreme Soup

SERVES 4

2 leeks, sliced (white and light green parts only)
20 asparagus spears, chopped
1 T. oil
32 oz. chicken or vegetable stock
Salt and pepper, to taste
Cooking spray

Spray a large pot with cooking spray. Heat and add oil. Sauté leeks for 2 minutes. Add asparagus and sauté for 5 minutes. Add stock, salt and pepper. Cook on medium flame for 30 minutes. Let cool and blend with a stick blender.

Cauliflower Zucchini Soup

SERVES 4-6

1 lg. onion, peeled and chopped

4 lg. zucchinis (with peel), chopped

1 (16 oz.) bag frozen cauliflower

6 c. water

3 T. consommé (no MSG)

Salt and pepper, to taste

2 T. light mayonnaise

2 packets sweetener

Cooking spray

Spray a 4 qt. pot with cooking spray. Sauté onion and zucchini until onion is translucent. Add frozen cauliflower, water and consommé. Cooking on high flame, bring soup to a boil. Lower flame and cook for approximately 45 minutes. Let cool, add mayonnaise and sweetener, and blend with a stick blender.

This recipe comes from my good friend Deena. With its creamy texture, it's definitely a comfort food and one of my favorites.

Butternut Squash and Pear Soup

SERVES 6

½ Vidalia onion, peeled and chopped

1 T. oil

2 ripe Bartlett pears, peeled and diced

1 (24 oz.) bag butternut squash

1 lg. carrot, peeled and chopped

1 parsnip, peeled and chopped

32 oz. vegetable stock

½ tsp. salt

1 tsp. cumin

In a large pot, sauté chopped onion in oil until translucent. Add pears and cook for 1–2 minutes. Add vegetables and cook until soft, then add remaining ingredients. Bring to a boil, lower flame and cook for 1 hour.

Cauliflower and Smokey Pepper Soup

SERVES 10

4 red peppers

1 T. oil

1 onion, chopped

3 garlic cloves, chopped

1 (16 oz.) bag frozen cauliflower

8 c. pareve chicken flavor stock

½ tsp. smoked paprika

Cut peppers in half. De-seed and place skin-side up in a 9x13-inch pan. Broil until charred. Let cool and peel off skin. Heat oil in a medium pot. Sauté onion and garlic. Add peppers and cauliflower. Add chicken stock and paprika. Cook for 1 hour. Let cool and blend with a stick blender.

Chunky Tuscan Tomato Soup

SERVES 8-10

Low-calorie Low-fat Gluten-free Vegan Dairy-free

1 Spanish onion, diced

2 stalks celery, sliced

2 carrots, peeled and thinly sliced

1 zucchini, chopped

1 T. oil

1 (15 oz.) can navy beans, drained

4 T. tomato paste

1 (29 oz.) can diced tomatoes with juice

4 c. vegetable stock

2 garlic cubes

2 basil cubes

1 T. consommé (no MSG)

Salt and pepper, to taste

Sauté onions, celery, carrots, and zucchini in oil until soft. Add rest of ingredients. Bring soup to a boil, lower flame and simmer for 1 hour.

Cream of Mushroom Soup

SERVES 6-8

½ lg. Spanish onion, chopped

2 celery stalks, chopped

1 T. oil

1 box mushrooms, washed and sliced

1 box Baby Bella mushrooms, washed and sliced

32 oz. vegetable broth

2 c. unsweetened almond milk

Sauté onion and celery until soft (1–2 minutes) in oil in a large heated pot on medium flame. Add mushrooms and stir. Cook for an additional 2 minutes. Add broth and cook for 1 hour. Let cool, add almond milk and blend with a stick blender.

Hungarian Cherry Soup

SERVES 6

1 (15 oz.) can sour cherries with liquid
½ c. pourable sweetener
½ tsp. vanilla extract
4 c. water
Juice of ½ fresh lemon
2 eggs

Place all ingredients in a medium pot, except for eggs and ½ the liquid from the sour cherries. Cook until soup reaches a boil. Shut flame. While soup is hot, take a separate bowl and blend eggs with a stick blender. To prevent the hot soup from cooking and solidifying the eggs, drizzle ½ of the cherry liquid into the eggs and blend with a stick blender. Add mixture to soup pot, place into a sealed container and chill for several hours.

This soup brings back childhood memories of sizzling summer Shabbosim accompanied by this cold refreshing soup. Perfect for shalosh seudos! It's a favorite with kids and adults alike.

Chunky Vegetable Soup

SERVES 8

1 Spanish onion, chopped

3 garlic cloves, chopped

3 celery stalks, chopped

1 T. oil

3 carrots, peeled and chopped

1 leek, chopped (white and light green part only)

1 turnip, peeled and chopped

1 parsnip, peeled and chopped

1 zucchini, chopped

8 c. of water + 4 T. consommé (no MSG)

1 bunch dill

1 bunch parsley

Cooking spray

Spray a large pot with cooking spray. Add oil. Sauté onion, garlic and celery for 1–2 minutes. Add rest of vegetables (except dill and parsley). Mix and add water with consommé. Place dill and parsley in net bag. Add to soup. Cook on medium flame for approximately 1½ hours.

As I am writing this, it is a freezing cold winter day, and I am actually eating this soup. It's the perfect prescription for bad weather. Don't get me wrong — pureed soups are delicious but sometimes you need more. This recipe is a combination of my favorite vegetables, which come together in a perfect medley of satisfaction.

Creamy Winter White Soup

SERVES 8

1 onion, chopped

3 garlic cloves, chopped

1 leek, chopped (white and light green parts only)

1 T. oil

1 lg. turnip, peeled and chopped

1 lg. parsnip, peeled and chopped

1 (24 oz.) bag frozen cauliflower

6 c. vegetable stock

½ tsp. celery seed

Salt and pepper, to taste

1 c. unsweetened almond milk

Sauté onion, garlic and leek in oil in a large pot until soft. Add turnip, parsnip, cauliflower and vegetable stock. Season with celery seed, salt and pepper. Cook for 1 hour on medium flame. Let cool, add almond milk, and blend with a stick blender.

Garnish:

½ onion, chopped

1 (10 oz.) pkg. mushrooms, sliced

1 tsp. oil

¼ tsp. paprika

Salt, to taste

Sauté onion and mushrooms in oil until brown. Season with paprika and salt.

Crockpot Butternut Squash Soup

SERVES 6-8

1 onion, chopped
3 celery stalks, sliced
2 garlic cubes
3 c. butternut squash, peeled and cubed
3 carrots, peeled and chopped
6 c. vegetable stock
¼ tsp. nutmeg
Salt and pepper, to taste

Place all ingredients in a crockpot. Cook on low for 8 hours or on high for 5 hours.

It was one of those days ... you got a call from your son's school because ... or your boss needed to speak to you, and your husband left you a message that it's urgent you call him as soon as possible. You finally get home and just want to eat anything that has chocolate as the first ingredient!!!! But just as you enter the kitchen, a wonderful aroma is emanating from your crockpot, and you suddenly remember the soup you put up before work. And once again, all is well with the world.

Cucumber Soup

SERVES 4

1 onion, peeled and chopped

1 T. lite trans fat–free spread

1 parsnip, peeled and chopped

4 Persian cucumbers, chopped

4 c. vegetable stock

½ c. unsweetened vanilla almond milk

Sauté onion in melted spread. Add parsnip, cucumbers and vegetable stock. Cook for 30 minutes on medium flame. Let cool, add almond milk and blend with a stick blender. Chill in refrigerator before serving.

Velvety Pea Soup

SERVES 6

1 shallot, chopped
2 celery stalks, chopped
2 leeks, chopped
1 T. oil
1 garlic cube
1 (16 oz.) bag frozen peas
¼ tsp. celery seed
½ tsp. salt
32 oz. chicken or vegetable stock
Cooking spray

Spray medium pot with cooking spray and add oil. Heat on medium flame until hot. Sauté shallot, celery and leeks for 2 minutes. Add garlic cube and peas and cook for another minute. Add celery seed, salt and stock and bring to a boil. Lower flame and cook for 40 minutes. Let cool and blend with a stick blender.

Pumpkin Soup

SERVES 6-8

1 T. oil
1 onion, chopped
2 garlic cloves, peeled and minced
2 carrots, peeled and chopped
1 (29 oz.) can pure pumpkin puree
6 c. water
2 T. consommé (no MSG)
Salt and pepper, to taste

Heat oil in a medium pot. Sauté onion, garlic and carrots for 1–2 minutes. Add pumpkin, water and consommé and cook for about 1 hour on low flame. Let cool and blend with a stick blender.

Roasted Cauliflower Leek Soup

SERVES 6

1 (24 oz.) bag frozen cauliflower

1 tsp. paprika

1 tsp. garlic

1 tsp. pepper

1 tsp. onion powder

2 celery stalks, chopped

2 leeks, chopped (white and light green parts only)

1 T. oil

1 tsp. salt

32 oz. chicken or pareve stock

Cooking spray

Place cauliflower in a 9x13-inch pan. Spray with cooking spray, and spice with paprika, garlic, pepper and onion powder. Bake at 400° uncovered for 1 hour. Heat oil in a medium pot. Sauté celery and leeks for 5 minutes. Add roasted cauliflower, stock and salt. Lower flame and simmer for approximately 30 minutes. Let cool and blend with a stick blender until smooth.

Tomato Soup with Shredded Zucchini

SERVES 6

2 lg. zucchini, shredded
1 T. oil
1 (46 oz.) can tomato juice
3 packets sweetener
Salt and pepper, to taste

Heat oil in a large pot. Add zucchini and sauté for about 2 minutes. Add tomato juice, sweetener and spices. Cook for 30 minutes.

Tomato Quinoa Soup

SERVES 6

1 T. oil

1 onion, peeled and chopped

2 garlic cloves, peeled and minced

2 celery stalks, chopped

1 basil cube

5 c. pareve chicken flavor or vegetable stock

1 (28 oz.) can plum tomato with basil

2 T. tomato paste

1 packet sweetener

½ tsp. garlic powder

Salt, to taste

1 c. cooked quinoa

Heat oil in a large pot. Add onion, garlic, celery and basil cube. Sauté vegetables for 1-2 minutes until soft. Add rest of ingredients (except cooked quinoa). Cook on medium flame for 45 minutes. Let cool and blend with a stick blender. Stir cooked quinoa into soup.

An updated and healthier version of the classic tomato and rice soup.

Zucchini Soup

SERVES 4-6

1 onion, chopped
3 garlic cubes
3 celery stalks, chopped
1 T. oil
3 lg. zucchini with peel, chopped
32 oz. pareve chicken flavor or vegetable stock
Salt and pepper, to taste
1 c. unsweetened almond milk

Sauté onion, garlic and celery in oil for 2-3 minutes. Add zucchini and cook for 2-3 minutes, stirring occasionally. Add stock, salt and pepper and cook for 1 hour on low flame. Let cool, add almond milk and blend with a stick blender.

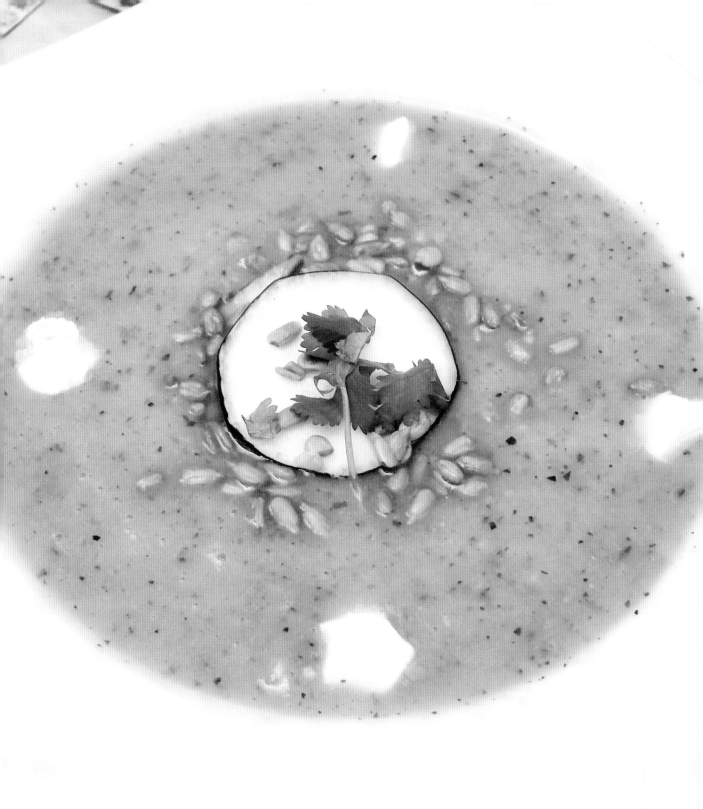

Side Dishes

Assorted Roasted Vegetables

SERVES 10-12

Assorted vegetables, such as:
Baby carrots, cut in half lengthwise
Eggplant, cut into half circles
Cauliflower florets
Zucchini, cut into circles
Red onions, cut into wedges
Assorted peppers, cut into thick strips
Brussels sprouts, cut into halves
Cooking spray

Dressing:
3 T. oil
1 T. red wine vinegar
1 garlic cube
1 tsp. spicy brown mustard
1 tsp. garlic pepper
1 tsp. paprika
1 tsp. onion powder
½ tsp. salt

Arrange vegetables in a single layer in four 9x13-inch pans. Spray vegetables with cooking spray. Mix dressing ingredients and drizzle over vegetables. Place in the oven (2 on the top rack and 2 on the bottom rack). Bake at 400° uncovered for 30 minutes. Switch the top rack pans to the bottom and vice versa. Bake uncovered for an additional 30 minutes.

Every Yom Tov I make trays of vegetables, using a variety of colors so it makes an eye pleasing dish. Unlike most roasted vegetable recipes, this one has a great dressing. Enjoy on Yom Tov and year round. Note: Some vegetables may take longer than others to cook.

Eggplant Medley

SERVES 6

Low-calorie　Low-fat　Low-carb　Vegan　Dairy-free　Passover

1 eggplant, cubed

1 green pepper, cut into strips

1 red pepper, cut into strips

1 red onion, cut into chunks

1 zucchini, sliced

1 T. oil

1 T. vinegar

1 packet sweetener

¼ tsp. onion powder

¼ tsp. garlic powder

Salt and pepper, to taste

Cooking spray

Place vegetables in a 9x13-inch pan greased with cooking spray. Combine oil, vinegar, sweetener and spices, and pour over vegetables. Bake at 400° covered for 1 hour.

Butternut Squash Risotto

SERVES 4-6

1 (24 oz.) pkg. frozen butternut squash, grated
2 tsp. oil
2 parsley cubes
¼ tsp. onion powder
¼ tsp. salt
1 c. vegetable stock

Heat pan with oil. Add butternut squash and sauté for 1 minute. Stir in parsley cubes, onion powder and salt. Add stock, lower flame and cook for 20 minutes.

This recipe is unlike any butternut squash recipe you have ever tasted. The grated squash and parsley give it an elegant look, making it a perfect dish for Shabbos or Yom Tov.

Broccoli and Brussels Sprouts

SERVES 8

2 garlic cloves, chopped

1 T. oil

1 sm. tomato, chopped

1 (24 oz.) bag broccoli florets, defrosted

8 Brussels sprouts, cut into halves

¼ tsp. salt

¼ tsp. pepper

In a medium pot, sauté garlic in oil. Add tomato and sauté for 1 minute. Add remaining ingredients and cook covered for 10 minutes on low flame.

Butternut Squash Hash Browns

SERVES 4

1 butternut squash, peeled and diced
½ lg. onion, diced
1 T. oil
½ tsp. salt
½ tsp. onion powder
½ tsp. garlic pepper
1 tsp. paprika
Cooking spray

Grease an oven-safe skillet with cooking spray. Place squash in a pan and add oil and onion. Sauté for 1 minute. Add spices and cook for 10 minutes. Put the skillet in the oven and bake at 350° uncovered for 40 minutes. Bake until soft, and crunchy on top.

This recipe is reminiscent of the breakfast special — soft on the inside, crunchy on top. The best part aside from the taste is that there's no time limit to eat them — you can make them even after 11 am.

Candied Butternut Squash

SERVES 6

5 c. butternut squash, cubed
Butter-flavored cooking spray
¼ c. sugar-free maple or pancake syrup
2 packets sweetener
¼ tsp. cinnamon

Place squash in a 9-inch round pan and spray with butter-flavored cooking spray. Mix remaining ingredients and drizzle on top of butternut squash. Bake at 400° uncovered for 1 hour (until squash is soft and top is brown).

This dish is so sweet and delicious it almost tastes like candy. I say "almost" because when I say "exactly," my kids ask me when was the last time I actually had candy! Okay, so you won't find this in the candy section of the grocery but if you're in the mood for something sweet while still eating vegetables, this recipe hits the spot.

Chinese Vegetables

SERVES 6

4 tsp. sesame oil
1 medium onion, chopped
2 garlic cloves, minced
1 red pepper, chopped
1 (3.5 oz.) box shiitake mushrooms, cleaned and cut into strips
1 (16 oz.) frozen bag oriental blend vegetables
1 (15 oz.) can cut baby corn
1 T. soy sauce
1 packet sweetener
¼ c. water
1 tsp. cornstarch
2 T. consommé (no MSG)

Heat a large pan with sesame oil until sizzling. Add onion, garlic and pepper, and cook for 2 minutes until soft. Add mushrooms, oriental vegetables, soy sauce and sweetener and cook for 5 minutes. Add baby corn and mix together. In a small bowl, stir cornstarch into water until diluted, then add consommé, mix well and add to pan. Cook for 20–30 minutes.

Nicer Dicer Chopped Zucchini and Mushrooms

SERVES 6

1 lg. zucchini
1 lg. yellow squash
1 box mushrooms
1 Vidalia onion
1½ T. oil
½ tsp. onion powder
½ tsp. salt
½ tsp. paprika
½ tsp. garlic pepper
Cooking spray

Chop all vegetables in a nicer dicer (can also be done by hand). Spray a large skillet with cooking spray, heat and add oil. Sauté onion for 2–3 minutes on medium flame. Add remaining vegetables and stir for a few minutes. Season with spices. Lower flame and cook for approximately 30 minutes (or until vegetables are soft).

Celery Root and Parsnip Mash

SERVES 6

1 lg. celery root, peeled and cut into chunks

3 parsnips, peeled and sliced

¼ c. unsweetened almond milk

½ tsp. salt

¼ tsp. garlic pepper

¼ tsp. paprika

Topping:
Sautéed onions

Place celery root and parsnips in a medium pot. Add water to cover and cook until soft. Cool, drain and place in a food processor with the S blade. Place remaining ingredients in the food processor and blend until smooth. Top with sautéed onions.

Garlic Broccoli with Cream Sauce

SERVES 4

Low-calorie · Low-fat · Vegan · Dairy-free

24 oz. frozen broccoli
3 garlic cloves, sliced
Cooking spray

Sauce:
2 T. Tofutti sour cream
½ T. red wine vinegar
½ tsp. mustard
Salt, to taste

Place broccoli and garlic in a 9x13-inch pan. Spray with cooking spray. Bake at 400° uncovered for 1 hour. Combine the sauce ingredients. Drizzle sauce on broccoli or serve on the side.

Garlic broccoli: good

Garlic broccoli with cream sauce: amazing!

Garlic Eggplant

SERVES 4

1 lg. Spanish onion, chopped

5 garlic cloves, minced

1 T. oil

2 plum tomatoes, chopped

1 lg. eggplant (with skin on), cubed

2 frozen parsley cubes

Salt and pepper, to taste

Cooking spray

Spray a medium pot with cooking spray. Add oil, onion, and garlic, and sauté until soft. Add tomatoes, eggplant and parsley cubes. Cook for 20 minutes on medium flame, and then season with salt and pepper.

Eggplant Ratatouille

SERVES 6

½ lg. onion, chopped

1 red pepper, chopped

1 T. olive oil

2 eggplants with skin on, cut into chunks

½ tsp. salt

½ tsp. garlic pepper

1 (16 oz.) can thick and spicy pizza sauce or tomato sauce

1 sweetener packet

Cooking spray

Grease a 4-quart pot with cooking spray. Add oil and heat on medium flame. Add onion and pepper and sauté for 2 minutes. Add eggplant and spices and continue cooking for 3 minutes. Add sauce and sweetener, mix thoroughly and then shut flame. Transfer to a 9x13-inch pan and bake at 400° covered for 1 hour.

I went through a phase when I had this every day for lunch. This recipe is one of the more hearty dishes, which makes it great for those winter months when you need a more filling and satisfying food. Add some protein, and you have a complete meal.

Honey Glazed String Beans

SERVES 6

3 garlic cloves

1 T. oil

1 red pepper, diced

16 oz. frozen French string beans, defrosted

¼ tsp. garlic pepper

¼ tsp. salt

¼ c. honey

1 tsp. soy sauce

2 tsp. cornstarch diluted with ½ c. cold water

Topping:

10 cashews, halved

Heat large pan, add oil and sauté garlic cloves until they begin to brown. Add diced red pepper and continue cooking for 3 minutes. Add string beans. Stir vegetables and cook for 5 minutes. Add rest of ingredients. Mix thoroughly and cook for an additional 5 minutes. Top with cashews right before serving.

Hot and Spicy Brussels Sprouts

SERVES 4

Low-calorie Low-fat Low-carb Gluten-free Vegan Dairy-free

1 (9 oz.) container Brussels sprouts
¼ tsp. sea salt (or kosher salt)
1 T. oil
Salt and pepper, to taste

Sauce:
3 T. hot sauce
2 T. water
4 tsp. honey
3 packets sweetener

Preheat oven to 350°. Trim Brussels sprouts and cut in half. In a medium pan, heat oil. Add Brussels sprouts and season with salt and pepper. Sauté for 2 minutes, then transfer to a 9-inch round dish. Mix sauce ingredients and pour over Brussels sprouts. Bake uncovered for 30 minutes.

Hot and Spicy Cauliflower

SERVES 4

1 (16 oz.) pkg. frozen cauliflower
3 T. hot sauce
¼ tsp. salt

Place cauliflower in a 9x13-inch pan. Drizzle with hot sauce and sprinkle with salt. Bake at 400° uncovered for 1 hour.

I created this recipe for the men who want, or should I say <u>need</u>, to eat healthier. I find that the men (at least the ones in my family) tend to eat anything as long as it has enough hot sauce.

Lemon Garlic Asparagus

SERVES 6-8

1 bunch fresh asparagus (about 35 spears)
2 tsp. oil
½ c. chicken broth (I prefer pareve)
2 garlic cubes
¼ tsp. salt
Squeeze of fresh lemon
Cooking spray

Cut bottom tips off asparagus and chop each spear into 3 pieces. Spray a large skillet with cooking spray and add oil. When heated, add asparagus and sauté for 5 minutes. Shut flame and place asparagus in a 9-inch round pan. Mix rest of ingredients and pour over asparagus. Bake at 350° covered for 20 minutes.

Tangy Portabella Mushrooms with Roasted Red Peppers

SERVES 4

1 box Baby Bella mushrooms, peeled and sliced

1½ red pepper, cut into strips

1 T. oil

1 T. soy sauce

Dressing:

2 T. olive oil

1 tsp. red wine vinegar

1 tsp. Dijon mustard

2 packets sweetener

Place vegetables in a 9x13-inch pan and drizzle with oil and soy sauce. Bake at 400°
uncovered for 30 minutes. Mix dressing ingredients, pour over vegetables and marinate
for 1 hour.

Marsala Mushrooms

SERVES 4-6

1 sm. onion, peeled and chopped
2 boxes sliced mushrooms
1 c. assorted mushrooms (Cremini, Portabella, and Shiitake)
1 T. oil
5 cubes parsley
3 T. Marsala cooking wine
¼ tsp. onion powder
¼ tsp. paprika
¼ tsp. salt
¼ tsp. pepper

Heat oil in a medium pot on low flame. Add onion and sauté for 1–2 minutes. Add mushrooms and continue sautéing until golden brown. Add parsley cubes, Marsala cooking wine and spices. Stir until mushrooms are fully cooked.

Cauliflower Rice

SERVES 6

1 (24 oz.) bag cauliflower, semi-defrosted
1 T. oil
1 (8 oz.) can mushrooms, drained
1 tsp. garlic powder
1 tsp. onion powder
1 tsp. salt
1 tsp. paprika

In a food processor (using grater disc), grate cauliflower till it resembles rice. Heat oil in a large pot, add cauliflower and mushrooms, and season with spices. Cook for 5 minutes until soft.

For those of you who follow low-carb diets and miss grains, this recipe is perfect. Due to the grating, the texture and taste will have you feel like you are eating rice but the scale will show otherwise!

Roasted Sesame Asparagus

SERVES 4-6

1 bunch of thin fresh asparagus spears, trimmed

1 T. sesame oil

1 T. soy sauce

1 T. sesame seeds

1 packet sweetener

Juice of ½ fresh lemon

Preheat oven to 400°. Place asparagus in a 9x13-inch pan. Mix rest of ingredients together and pour over asparagus, coating evenly. Bake uncovered for 20 minutes. Squirt with fresh lemon before serving.

Rutabaga French Fries

SERVES 4

1 lg. rutabaga
1 T. oil
¼ tsp. paprika
¼ tsp. onion powder
¼ tsp. garlic pepper
Cooking spray

Put rutabaga in a microwave on high for 3-5 minutes. Peel and cut evenly into strips. Place rutabaga fries on a cookie sheet. Spray fries with cooking spray, then drizzle oil on top. Add spices, then bake at 400° uncovered for 1 hour.

Let's face it. When we are told to eat healthier and add vegetables to our diet, we think "bland, boring and basic." My goal is to change that to fun and great tasting. That was not a typo — you read correctly. Rutabaga is one of those root vegetables that work very well as a substitute for potatoes. Besides, any recipe with the word "fries" in it has to taste delicious. Pair these fries with your favorite veggie burger for a complete meal!

Sautéed Spinach

SERVES 4

4 garlic cloves, thinly sliced
1 T. olive oil
1 (20 oz.) pkg. fresh spinach
1 T. fresh lemon juice
¼ tsp. salt
¼ tsp. crushed red pepper

Heat oil in a skillet over medium flame and add garlic. Cook until slightly brown. Lower flame, add spinach and toss with garlic. Cover and cook until wilted (3-5 minutes). Remove from flame. Add rest of ingredients, mix well and serve immediately.

Sesame Celery

SERVES 2

1 pkg. celery stalks, chopped (approximately 3 cups)
5 garlic cloves, chopped
1 T. sesame oil
1 T. soy sauce
1 T. sesame seeds
Salt and pepper, to taste

Heat oil in a skillet, and add celery and garlic. Sauté for 1-2 minutes, then add rest of ingredients. Cook for an additional 5-7 minutes until celery is soft.

Celery is known as a negative calorie food. That means that it takes more calories to chew it than it contains. Most people only think of celery as raw and cut into sticks (usually partnered with carrot sticks). This recipe allows you to enjoy the cooked version.

Sesame Zoodles

SERVES 4

3 sm. or 1 jumbo zucchini (should amount to 5 c. of zoodles)
4 tsp. sesame seeds
2 scallions, chopped

Dressing:
4 tsp. smooth peanut butter
1 T. water
1 tsp. sesame oil
½ T. honey
Squeeze of fresh lime
Salt, to taste

Place zucchini in a spiralizer, forming noodles (can use a Julienne peeler, but the texture is different). Place zucchini in a medium bowl. Sprinkle with sesame seeds and add scallions. Combine dressing ingredients. Mix well until blended, pour on top of noodles and toss.

The best part of making a cookbook is tasting all these scrumptious new recipes. Since it's a low-calorie cookbook, instead of gaining weight I lost — a win-win! This is one of my new favorites.

Sundried Tomatoes

SERVES 4-6

3 beefsteak tomatoes, thinly sliced
2 tsp. salt
2 tsp. oregano
4 garlic cubes
4 basil cubes
¼ c. olive oil

Place tomatoes in two 9x13-inch pans. Sprinkle salt and oregano over tomatoes. Mix garlic, basil and oil in a small bowl. Pour over tomatoes. Bake at 250° uncovered for 2 hours.

This recipe is worth making just for the smell that will waft through your house. Of course, it also tastes delicious! Whether you eat this plain or on top of crackers, this homemade version is way healthier and better-tasting than the store-bought kind.

Shredded Kohlrabi and Carrots

SERVES 2-4

2 medium kohlrabi, peeled and shredded
2 lg. carrots, peeled and shredded
1 T. oil
Salt and pepper, to taste

Heat oil in a medium pot. Add kohlrabi, carrots, salt and pepper. Cook for 20 minutes, stirring occasionally until tender.

Sweet and Sour Cabbage

SERVES 4

1 onion, chopped
1 (16 oz.) bag coleslaw mix
¼ tsp. salt
¼ tsp. paprika
¼ tsp. garlic pepper
1 (8 oz.) can tomato sauce
2 packets sweetener
Cooking spray

In a large pot, sauté onion in cooking spray for 1 minute. Add coleslaw mix and spices. (You may need to add more cooking spray.) Cook for 10 minutes, stirring occasionally. Add tomato sauce and sweetener, and continue to cook for 20 minutes.

Sweet and Sour Vegetables

SERVES 4

1 c. onions, chopped

1 c. mushrooms, sliced

1 green pepper, cut into strips

½ c. carrots, chopped

½ c. celery, chopped

1 T. soy sauce

½ c. crushed pineapple with juice

1 T. oil

Heat oil in a large skillet. Add all the vegetables, stirring till mostly soft but still a bit crunchy. Add soy sauce and pineapple. Stir for about a minute until all ingredients are combined.

This recipe is interesting because of the combination of fruit and vegetables. Usually that combination is found in salads, not cooked vegetables. The tanginess of the pineapple really pairs well with the savory vegetables.

Tomato and Basil Spinach

SERVES 8

1 Spanish onion, chopped
1 T. oil
½ box grape tomatoes, sliced in half
1 box mushrooms, peeled and sliced
3 garlic cubes
3 basil cubes
1 (2 lb.) bag frozen chopped spinach, defrosted and excess water removed
½ tsp. salt
½ tsp. garlic pepper
Cooking spray

Grease a 4-quart pot with cooking spray, add oil and heat. Add onion and sauté for about a minute. Add tomatoes, mushrooms, garlic and basil. Cook for 5-7 minutes until mushrooms are soft. Add spinach and spices. Mix well, lower flame and cook for approximately 8-10 minutes.

While on vacation in L.A., I tried this dish in a little café. As soon as I got home, I played around with the ingredients to try and duplicate it. Nailed it! Now I can make it anytime at home (though there's something nice about having it served to you ....)

Sweet and Spicy Carrot Fries

SERVES 4-6

6 carrots, cut into sticks

½ tsp. garlic powder

½ tsp. cinnamon

½ tsp. cayenne pepper

½ tsp. sea salt (or kosher salt)

1 packet sweetener

2 T. oil

Preheat oven to 350°. Place all ingredients in a tightly sealed plastic bag and shake until coated. Arrange on a cookie sheet and bake uncovered for 45 minutes.

Citrus Shredded Carrots

SERVES 6

4 lg. carrots, shredded
1 T. oil
Butter-flavored cooking spray
2 T. lemon juice
½ c. lite orange juice
3 packets sweetener

Spray medium pot with butter-flavored cooking spray. Add carrots and oil and mix for 1-2 minutes. Add rest of ingredients. Cover and cook on low flame for 20 minutes or until soft.

This is my mother-in-law's recipe. When I was first married, she always used to make this for me because it was my favorite. (I think she was happy someone actually enjoyed her vegetables, since she only has boys!) The original recipe uses regular orange juice, but I substituted light OJ to give it less sugar — but with the same great taste!

Matchstick Vegetables

SERVES 4

1 lg. carrot
1 lg. zucchini
1 lg. yellow squash
1 red pepper
2 stalks celery
2 tsp. oil
Salt and pepper, to taste

Julienne-cut all vegetables into matchsticks. Heat oil in a pan on medium flame and then add vegetables. Stir vegetables and add salt and pepper. Lower flame and cook for 20 minutes, stirring occasionally.

Tzimmes

SERVES 8

1 (16 oz.) bag frozen sliced carrots
1 (15 oz.) can pineapple chunks (in juice)
2 T. craisins
2 tsp. cornstarch
½ tsp. cinnamon
5 packets sweetener

In a medium pot, cook carrots in water until soft. Drain carrots and return to the pot. Drain pineapple chunks, saving the juice. Add pineapple and craisins to the pot. Dilute cornstarch in pineapple juice. Pour into the pot, and then add cinnamon and sweetener. Cook for 30 minutes.

Tzimmes is one of those underrated foods that just sit in the showcase at the takeout, looking all lonely and silently begging to be bought. Maybe it's the prunes ... This recipe is light and sweet and, best of all, not a prune in sight!

Zucchini in Tomato Sauce

SERVES 4

½ lg. Vidalia onion, chopped
1 T. oil
2 medium green zucchini, sliced
1 medium yellow zucchini, sliced
1 (15 oz.) can tomato sauce
½ tsp. salt
3 packets sweetener
Cooking spray

Spray a medium pot with cooking spray. Add oil and sauté onion for 1 minute. Add zucchini and squash and continue to sauté for another 10-15 minutes. Add tomato sauce, salt and sweetener. Cook for 30 minutes.

Kugels

Broccoli Lukshen Kugel

SERVES 6

1 c. chopped frozen broccoli

¼ onion, chopped and sautéed in cooking spray

1 c. cooked thin whole-wheat noodles

1 c. cooked spaghetti squash

3 egg whites

2 T. light mayonnaise

1 T. onion soup mix (no MSG)

Salt and pepper, to taste

Cooking spray

In a large bowl, mix all ingredients together. Place in an 8x8-inch pan greased with cooking spray. Bake at 350° uncovered for 1 hour until firm.

This recipe comes from my cooking aficionado friend Karen. That means it's a winner!

Butternut Squash Kugel

SERVES 4-6

1 (24 oz.) bag diced frozen butternut squash, cooked
¼ c. unsweetened almond milk
1 egg and 1 egg white
¼ tsp. vanilla extract
¼ tsp. cinnamon
2 T. sugar-free maple syrup
1 T. sweetener
¼ tsp. salt

Topping:
Butter-flavored cooking spray
Cinnamon and sweetener, for dusting

Place butternut squash in a microwave and cook according to package directions. Place squash in a bowl and mash. Add rest of ingredients and mix thoroughly. Place in a 9-inch round pan. Spray butter-flavored spray on top. Dust with cinnamon and sweetener. Bake at 400° uncovered for 50 minutes.

Obviously, I'm obsessed with butternut squash. I especially love butternut squash kugel, but all the recipes I found were full of sugar and fat. Now you can enjoy my lightened up version — I got rid of the sugar and fat but kept all the taste.

California Kugel

SERVES 12

1 (24 oz.) bag California blend vegetables, defrosted
1 (24 oz.) bag diced butternut squash, defrosted
3 egg whites, beaten
1 Spanish onion, chopped and sautéed
2 T. light mayonnaise
1 tsp. salt
¼ tsp. onion powder
¼ tsp. garlic pepper
¼ tsp. paprika

In a large pot, cook vegetables in water until soft. Drain any liquid and mash vegetables. Add remaining ingredients and mix thoroughly. Place in a 9x13-inch pan and bake at 400° uncovered for 1 hour.

I came up with this recipe on Pesach. Most recipes for Pesach have potato or potato starch. Not this one — instead, I used butternut squash. It works well with the California blend and makes a nice amount of servings. (Who knows? Maybe this Pesach you'll actually lose weight!)

Cauliflower Kugel

SERVES 12

2 (24 oz.) bags cauliflower, cooked
1 Vidalia onion, chopped and sautéed
1 egg and 2 egg whites
1 tsp. salt
2 T. oil
Cooking spray

Spray a 9x13-inch pan with cooking spray, add oil, and heat the pan in the oven at 400°
until sizzling. In a bowl, mash cooked cauliflower, and then add remaining ingredients
and mix. Transfer to the pan and bake at 400° uncovered for 1 hour.

This is my version of potato kugel — it's low in calories and carbs and has way less
fat than most potato kugel recipes. The only thing not missing is taste! Now you can
enjoy your kugel on Shabbos and not feel deprived.

Cauliflower Butternut Squash Kugel

SERVES 8-10

1 (24 oz.) bag frozen cauliflower
1 (24 oz.) bag frozen butternut squash
1 red onion, chopped
3 egg whites
1 T. light mayonnaise
¼ tsp. garlic pepper
¼ tsp. onion powder
½ tsp. salt
Cooking spray

In a large pot, cook cauliflower and butternut squash until soft. Drain and mash. In a small skillet, sauté onion in cooking spray until soft. Add to cauliflower and butternut squash mixture. Add rest of ingredients and mix thoroughly. Transfer to a 9x13-inch pan. Bake at 400° uncovered for 1 hour.

This recipe was created due to overcrowding in my freezer! I took out bags of frozen vegetables and voila! This creation was born.

Pineapple Noodle Kugel

SERVES 6

1 c. cooked spaghetti squash
1 c. cooked thin whole-wheat noodles
3 egg whites
2 T. craisins
2 T. light mayonnaise
½ c. crushed pineapple, drained (as best as possible)
¼ tsp. cinnamon
½ tsp. vanilla extract
¼ tsp. salt

Combine all ingredients in a medium bowl and mix thoroughly. Place in an 8½ x 4½-inch loaf pan. Bake at 350° uncovered for 1 hour.

Pumpkin Pineapple Kugel

SERVES 6

1 (15 oz.) can pure pumpkin puree
½ c. crushed pineapple (in juice)
1 egg plus 1 egg white
⅓ c. unsweetened vanilla almond milk
¼ tsp. pumpkin pie spice
¼ tsp. cinnamon
1 T. pourable sweetener
Butter-flavored cooking spray

Preheat oven to 350°. Mix all ingredients in a medium bowl. Pour into a 9-inch round pan and spray the top with butter-flavored cooking spray. Bake uncovered for 1 hour until firm.

Zucchini Kugel

SERVES 6-8

1 (24 oz.) bag frozen yellow zucchini

1 (24 oz.) bag frozen green zucchini

1 (8 oz.) can mushrooms

1 T. light mayonnaise

1 sm. onion, chopped and sautéed

1 egg plus 1 additional egg white, beaten together

½ tsp. salt

½ tsp. garlic pepper

½ tsp. onion powder

½ tsp. garlic powder

Preheat oven to 400°. Place a frozen yellow and green squash in a pot and cook on low flame. Drain and place in a bowl. Lightly mash with a fork. Add rest of ingredients and mix. Place kugel mixture into a 9-inch round pan. Bake uncovered for 45 minutes to 1 hour until golden.

Shredded Apple Kugel

SERVES 4

4 baking apples, shredded
4 egg whites
¼ tsp. vanilla extract
1 ½ T. pourable sweetener
½ tsp. cinnamon
Juice of ½ fresh lemon

In a medium bowl, mix all ingredients. Place in a 9-inch round pan. Bake at 350°
uncovered for 1 hour.

Spinach "Lukshen" Kugel

SERVES 6

2 lb. spaghetti squash

1 sm. onion, chopped

1 (32 oz.) bag frozen spinach, defrosted and drained

1 egg plus 3 egg whites

1 T. consommé (no MSG)

½ tsp. salt

Pinch of black pepper

Cooking spray

Cut spaghetti squash lengthwise in half and place both halves flat side down in a 9x13-inch pan. Bake for 1 hour at 400°. Cool, then separate strands from peel with a fork. Set aside. In a large pot, sauté onion in cooking spray until translucent. Shut flame, add spinach to the pot and mix with onions. Add spaghetti squash strands, eggs, consommé, salt and pepper. Mix thoroughly. Place in a 10-inch round pan and bake at 400° uncovered for 1 hour until firm.

Snacks

Baked Apple Chips

SINGLE SERVING

1 large baking apple
Butter-flavored or regular cooking spray
1 packet sweetener
Cinnamon

Spray a cookie sheet with cooking spray. Peel and cut apple into ¼ inch slices. Place on the cookie sheet. Spray apple slices with butter-flavored cooking spray. Sprinkle sweetener and cinnamon on top. Bake at 200° uncovered. For softer consistency, bake for 2 hours. For chewier consistency, bake for an additional 20 minutes.

This recipe can be doubled or tripled, but be careful — they're addictive!

Carrot Crisps

SINGLE SERVING

2 lg. carrots, peeled
Butter-flavored cooking spray
¼ tsp. cinnamon
2 packets sweetener

Preheat oven to 200°. Using a spiralizer or Julienne peeler, cut carrots. Place carrots on a cookie sheet and spray with butter-flavored spray. Sprinkle cinnamon and sweetener on top. Bake at 200° uncovered for approximately 2 hours. (If you used a Julienne peeler, check after 1½ hours.)

These carrot crisps are sweet and crunchy and make a perfect snack for kids — assuming you don't finish them all yourself!

Chocolate Halva Treats

YIELD: 12

1 c. melted sugar-free pareve chocolate chips
12 tsp. tehina paste

Take one teaspoon melted chocolate and spoon into each section of a mini muffin pan. Spread chocolate onto bottom and sides. Add 1 teaspoon tehina paste, and then cover with one teaspoon chocolate. Put into freezer until firm.

I am all about health and fruits and vegetables (hence this cookbook), but I'm also human and sometimes a girl just needs her chocolate. When that time comes, you'll be prepared. These little halva treats are a mini lower-calorie version of the original and taste just as sinful — but without the guilt!

Blueberry Chia Pudding

SINGLE SERVING

1 c. frozen blueberries, defrosted

¾ c. of unsweetened vanilla almond milk

3 packets sweetener

¼ tsp. vanilla extract

2 T. chia seeds

Mix all ingredients in a small bowl. Chill in refrigerator for 2 hours until it forms a pudding-like consistency.

Cinnamon Apple Snack

SINGLE SERVING

1 lg. apple, peeled and chopped using dicer chopper
(can also be done by hand)
Juice of ½ fresh lemon
¼ tsp. vanilla extract
1 packet sweetener
¼ tsp. cinnamon
Butter–flavored cooking spray

Spray a large skillet with butter-flavored cooking spray and add apples. Stir for about a minute, and then add rest of ingredients. Stir constantly on low flame, until soft.

This has the same caloric value as eating an apple but the difference is whether you'll be eating an apple or eating a dessert. The choice is up to you.

Coconut Pineapple Kisses

YIELD: 24

1 (20 oz.) can crushed pineapple (in juice)
3 egg whites
½ c. unsweetened shredded coconut
½ tsp. vanilla extract
¼ c. pourable sweetener

In a non-stick skillet, heat crushed pineapple with juice until juice is evaporated. Cook, stirring constantly until pineapple is sticky and begins to caramelize. Remove from heat. In a large mixing bowl, combine egg whites, coconut, vanilla and sweetener. Add pineapple and mix well. Preheat oven to 375°. To shape each kiss, spoon 1 tablespoon of mixture onto a parchment-lined cookie sheet. With your fingers, gently pull center up to form a kiss. Bake 30 minutes until lightly golden. Cool before serving.

This heavenly recipe is a cross between a cookie and candy. The caramelized pineapple and chewy coconut will make it feel like there's a party in your mouth.

Dairy-free Peanut Butter Cups

YIELD: 12

1 c. melted sugar-free pareve chocolate chips
4 T. peanut butter

Using a small spoon, coat each section of a mini muffin pan with 1 tsp. melted chocolate. Add 1 tsp. peanut butter over chocolate. Carefully add 1 tsp. chocolate to cover peanut butter. Cover and freeze overnight.

Chocolate and peanut butter — need I say more? Actually I could always say more. What I will say is that this recipe is excellent for anyone who can't have dairy but dreams of chocolate peanut butter cups.

Scrumptious Chocolate Chip Cookies

YIELD: 24

1 (15 oz.) can chickpeas or any white beans
2 T. peanut butter
1 tsp. vanilla extract
¾ tsp. baking powder
1 pinch baking soda
2 T. sugar-free maple syrup
2 T. sweetener
1 T. unsweetened applesauce
¼ tsp. cinnamon
1 pinch of salt
Cooking spray

Topping:
Sugar-free pareve chocolate chips

Mix all ingredients in a food processor with S blade until smooth. Grease a cookie sheet with cooking spray. Place heaping tablespoon of batter onto the cookie sheet. Place chocolate chips onto each cookie. Bake 30-40 minutes at 350° until firm.

No, I was not delirious when I wrote this recipe! Before you dismiss this — try it. Not only are these cookies healthy and delicious, they are also chock full of protein.

Melt-in-Your-Mouth Brownies

SERVES 6

1 c. sugar-free chocolate chips, melted

1 sm. ripe banana

2 T. peanut butter

1 tsp. vanilla extract

1 pinch of salt

3 T. cocoa

¼ c. sugar-free maple syrup

Preheat oven to 350°. Blend all ingredients in a food processor with S blade. Grease an 8x8-inch pan. Pour batter into pan and bake uncovered for approximately 40 minutes.

Allergic to eggs? Can't have gluten? Crave a snack but can't look at another rice cake? This fudge brownie is the perfect treat for you!

Fat-Free Apple Cinnamon Muffins

YIELD: 12

1½ c. whole-wheat blend flour

½ c. oats

1 yellow apple, peeled and chopped into pieces

1 egg

½ c. apple juice

2 T. unsweetened applesauce

1 c. pourable sweetener

¼ tsp. cinnamon

1 tsp. vanilla

¾ tsp. baking soda

2 tsp. baking powder

¼ tsp. salt

In a large bowl, mix all ingredients together by hand. Spoon into 12 sprayed muffin tins. Bake at 375° for 20 minutes.

The most popular request I got when I mentioned I was doing a cookbook was for a low-calorie muffin. The real question is: Why do we call it a "cupcake" when we are eating unhealthy, but when we're watching what we eat we call it a "muffin"? Well, whether you call it a cupcake or a muffin, one thing's for sure — it's delicious!

Low-carb Almond Cookies

YIELD: 8

1 c. slivered almonds
2 egg whites
3 T. sweetener
¼ tsp. cinnamon
¼ tsp. vanilla extract

Mix all ingredients in a medium bowl. Spray a cookie sheet with cooking spray. Form batter into 8 cookies and place on the cookie sheet. Bake at 350° for about 20 minutes, until lightly golden.

This recipe comes from my neighbor ZC, whose husband is the leading authority on low-carb eating. (People on my block do not eat carbs in front of him.)

Vanilla Meringue Cookies

YIELD: 18

3 egg whites
3 packets sweetener
¼ tsp. vanilla extract
¼ tsp. cream of tartar
1 T. sugar-free vanilla pudding

With a mixer on high, beat egg whites. Slowly add rest of ingredients. Continue beating for a few minutes until stiff. Place mixture into a Ziploc bag. Cut the bottom corner of the bag to create a pastry bag. Pipe cookies onto a parchment-lined cookie sheet. Bake at 200° for about 1 hour until firm. (For chocolate meringues, use sugar-free chocolate instant pudding powder instead of vanilla.)

Sweet Potato Chips

SERVES 4

2 lg. sweet potatoes
¼ tsp. paprika
¼ tsp. salt
¼ tsp. onion powder
¼ tsp. garlic powder
Cooking spray

With a mandolin or food processor, slice sweet potatoes into very thin rounds. Place on a cookie sheet, spray generously with cooking spray and sprinkle spices evenly. Bake at 200° for 2 hours, and then raise temperature to 300° for 30 minutes. Check on chips every so often to prevent over baking.

Desserts

Apple Meringue

SINGLE SERVING

Low-calorie · Low-fat · Gluten-free · Sugar-free · Dairy-free · Passover

1 apple, peeled and thinly sliced
Butter-flavored cooking spray
¼ tsp. cinnamon
1 packet sweetener
1 T. sugar-free apricot jelly

Place apple slices in an 8x8-inch pan. Spray with butter-flavored cooking spray. Place rest of ingredients on top of apples. Set aside.

Meringue:
2 egg whites
¼ tsp. cinnamon
¼ tsp. vanilla
2 packets sweetener
2 T. unsweetened applesauce
1 tsp. sugar-free apricot jelly

Preheat oven to 350°. Beat egg whites in a medium bowl until they are stiff and form peaks. Fold in rest of ingredients. Spoon meringue over apples. Bake uncovered for 30 minutes until top is golden brown.

Apple Pear Crisp

SERVES 4

2 lg. Cortland apples, peeled and sliced
2 ripe Bosc pears, peeled and sliced
Pinch of cinnamon
1 packet sweetener

Crumb Recipe:
4 T. whole-wheat blend flour
4 T. oats
¼ tsp. cinnamon
1½ T. oil
4 packets sweetener

Place apples and pears in a 9-inch round pan. Sprinkle with cinnamon and sweetener.
In a small bowl, mix crumb ingredients with a fork. Crumble on top of apples and pears.
Bake at 350° uncovered for 45 minutes until soft.

Apple Pie with Biscotti Crumbs

SERVES 8

4 lg. Cortland apples, peeled and sliced

Butter-flavored cooking spray

½ tsp. cinnamon

1 tsp. vanilla extract

3 packets sweetener

8 low-calorie biscotti (cinnamon or vanilla flavor work best)

Layer the apples flat in a 9x13-inch pan. Spray butter-flavored cooking spray over apples. Drizzle vanilla and sprinkle sweetener and cinnamon on top. In a tightly sealed Ziploc bag, using a mallet, crush biscotti into crumbs. Sprinkle on top of apples and spray butter-flavored cooking spray on crumbs. Bake at 350° uncovered for 40 minutes.

I couldn't decide whether to list this recipe as a kugel or a dessert. Yup — it's that delicious and that versatile. You decide!

Banana Cake

SERVES 2

½ pkg. firm tofu
1 ripe banana
2 egg whites
6 packets sweetener
½ tsp. vanilla

Place all ingredients in a food processor with S blade. Mix until it has a creamy consistency. Place in an 8x8-inch pan. Bake at 350° uncovered for 30 minutes.

Optional: While still hot, sprinkle 1 tsp. of sugar-free chocolate chips and press down lightly (which allows them to melt slightly).

Blueberry Apple Pie

SERVES 6

4 green apples, peeled and sliced
Cinnamon
1 (16 oz.) bag frozen blueberries

Arrange apple slices in a 10-inch round dish. Sprinkle cinnamon on top. Place blueberries on top of apples, cover and tightly seal with foil. Bake at 350° covered for 1 hour until soft.

Whenever guests ask me for the recipe for this dessert, they are always surprised that it's just fruit. The taste has richness that feels like something more.

Apple Strudel

SERVES 6

Low-calorie Low-fat Sugar-free Vegan Dairy-free

3 sheets phyllo dough
Pinch of cinnamon
Butter-flavored cooking spray

Filling:
2 yellow apples, peeled and very thinly sliced
½ tsp. vanilla extract
1 T. sugar-free apricot jelly
1 T. sugar-free maple syrup
¼ tsp. cinnamon
1 packet sweetener

Combine all filling ingredients in a medium bowl. On a clean dishtowel, unroll phyllo dough. Gently remove 3 sheets and carefully place them on a greased cookie sheet. Spoon filling along the length of phyllo dough, and then evenly roll into jelly roll shape. Sprinkle the top with a pinch of cinnamon and then spray with butter-flavored cooking spray. Bake at 350° uncovered for 40–50 minutes or until golden brown.

The number one reason people go back to their old unhealthy eating habits is deprivation. So I took some dessert favorites and gave them a makeover. This strudel is flaky on the outside, moist and sweet on the inside. You won't feel deprived with this recipe.

Crustless Strawberry Cream Pie

SERVES 4-6

4 c. strawberries, sliced
1 box sugar-free vanilla instant pudding mix
1½ c. unsweetened vanilla almond milk
1 T. Tofutti cream cheese
2 packets sweetener

Arrange strawberries in a 9-inch round pan and set aside. In a mixer, beat rest of ingredients. Pour over strawberries. Refrigerate for 2-4 hours until set.

Honey-Drizzled Peaches with Crunchy Oat Topping

SERVES 6

6 peaches, cut into chunks

1 T. honey

½ tsp. vanilla extract

2 packets sweetener

Oat Topping (bake separately to keep from getting soggy):

¾ c. oats

¼ c. slivered almonds (toasted in butter-flavored cooking spray)

4 tsp. oil

1 egg white

¼ tsp. cinnamon

¼ tsp. vanilla

2 T. pourable sweetener

Pinch of salt

Place peaches in a 9x13-inch pan. Mix honey, vanilla extract and sweetener and pour over peaches. Bake at 350° uncovered for 30-40 minutes. Mix all topping ingredients together in a small bowl. Place in an 8x8-inch pan and bake at 350° uncovered for 20 minutes. Spoon on top of peaches (can also be used for any other fruit dessert).

Mango Ices

SERVES 8

1 (16 oz.) bag frozen mango, semi-defrosted
6 packets sweetener
1 c. diet mango juice
Juice of ½ fresh lemon
Juice of ½ fresh lime

Blend ingredients in a food processor until it has a creamy consistency. Pour into a sealed container. Freeze for several hours or overnight.

My entire family loves this recipe — and that's a big deal. In my house, no one agrees on anything when it comes to food. It's nice to know that at least there's one thing they all enjoy!

Pina Colada Granita

SERVES 4

2 c. crushed pineapple, drained (as best as possible)
2 egg whites
3 packets sweetener
¼ tsp. coconut extract

Place all ingredients in a food processor with S blade. Beat until egg whites are frothy. Place in a container and freeze overnight.

Need a vacation but can't get away? With my pina colada granita, you'll feel like you're on some tropical getaway (at least until the kids start fighting).

Plum Tart

SERVES 4-6

4 sheets phyllo dough
Butter-flavored cooking spray
4 ripe plums, cut into wedges
1 packet sweetener
2 T. orange juice

On a clean dishtowel, unroll phyllo dough. Gently remove 4 sheets and place on a cookie sheet. Spray dough lightly with butter-flavored cooking spray. Arrange plum wedges in rows on dough. Slightly fold long sides first, then shorter sides (forming a frame around the wedges). Drizzle juice and sprinkle sweetener over plums. Bake at 350° uncovered for 20-30 minutes until brown.

Rich and Creamy Chocolate Mousse

SERVES 2

1 ripe avocado

1 lg. banana

2 T. cocoa

¼ c. unsweetened almond milk

¼ tsp. vanilla extract

3 packets sweetener

Place all ingredients in a food processor, blend until smooth, and serve.

Strawberry Mousse

SINGLE SERVING

Low-calorie · Sugar-free · Fat-free · Gluten-free · Dairy-free · Passover

1½ c. sliced strawberries
1 egg white
2 packets sweetener

Place all ingredients in a food processor with S blade. Blend for about 5 minutes until mousse is a whipped consistency. Serve immediately.

Strawberry Blueberry "Pie"

SERVES 6

1 (16 oz.) bag frozen blueberries

1 (16 oz.) bag frozen strawberries

1 T. sweetener

1 T. cornstarch

½ T. lemon zest

Topping:

1 whole-wheat 90-calorie tortilla

Butter-flavored cooking spray

Cinnamon and sweetener

Mix all "pie" ingredients in a medium bowl. Place in a 9-inch round pan. Bake at 350°
uncovered for 45 minutes. Cut tortilla into strips and then place strips on a cookie sheet.
Spray with buttered-flavored cooking spray. Sprinkle with cinnamon and sweetener.
Bake at 350° uncovered for 10 minutes. Let cool, then use strips to form lattice on top
of pie.

What says summer more than a berry pie?

Strawberry Rhubarb Compote

SERVES 6

1 (16 oz.) bag frozen strawberries
   with rhubarb

4 c. water

3 Cortland apples, peeled and cut into chunks

1 T. sugar-free cherry jello

Place all ingredients in a medium pot. Cook for 30 minutes on medium flame. Let cool and chill in refrigerator for 2 hours.

Vanilla Fudge Ice Cream

SERVES 2

2 frozen bananas, peeled and chopped
(peel before you freeze)

1 T. cocoa

2 packets sweetener

¼ tsp. vanilla extract

¼ c. unsweetened almond milk

Place all ingredients in a food processor. Blend until it has a smooth and creamy texture.

Ice cream lovers (with milk allergies) — rejoice! This recipe is also great for vegans.

Mini Sweet Potato Soufflés

SERVES 6

2 baked sweet potatoes, peeled and mashed (approx. 2 cups)

1 tsp. trans fat-free pareve spread

2 T. sugar-free maple syrup

2 egg whites

¼ c. orange juice

4 packets sweetener

¼ tsp. cinnamon

Topping:

6 T. corn flake crumbs

¼ tsp. cinnamon

Butter-flavored cooking spray

Mix all soufflé ingredients in a medium bowl. Pour batter into 6 mini oven-safe ramekins. Combine topping ingredients, divide into six portions and sprinkle on top of soufflés. Spray butter-flavored cooking spray on topping and bake at 350° uncovered for 30 minutes.